Table of Contents

INTRODUCTION 4
    The Hamburger Stand And How Ray Kroc Joined The Company 5
MCDONALD'S PRODUCT MIX 7
    Unique international menu items 8
    Product in the Marketing mix of McDonalds 9
    Price in the Marketing mix of McDonalds 9
    Promotions in the Marketing mix of McDonalds 10
    Place in the Marketing mix of McDonalds 11
    People in the Marketing mix of McDonalds 11
    Process in the Marketing mix if McDonalds 11
    Physical evidence in the Marketing mix of McDonalds 12
    MCDONALD'S CROSS-SELLING 13
    MCDONALD'S UP-SELLING 13
MCDONALD'S CORPORATE REALITY 15
    COUNTRIES WITH MCDONALD'S 15
    A Symbol Of Globalization 19
BUSINESS STRATEGY OF MCDONALD'S 20
    How Much Is McDonald's Really Worth? 23
    Ray Kroc Net Worth 25
REAL ESTATE OR HAMBURGER 26
MCDONALD'S FRANCHISING 32
    McDonald's Franchises 34
    Location Requirements 35
    Facility Considerations 35
MCDONALD'S LAYOUT, PROCESS TYPE AND USE OF TECHNOLOGIES 36
LEADERSHIP OF RAY KROC 43
MCDONALD'S PRODUCTS CONSISTENCY 47
HOW MCDONALD'S BUILD ITS SUSTAINABLE COMPETITIVE ADVANTAGE? -THE KEY SUCCESS FACTORS AND BUSINESS STRATEGY 50

THE FUTURE OF MCDONALD'S 72
CONCLUSION 74

INTRODUCTION

The first McDonald's restaurant was started in 1948 by brothers Maurice ("Mac") and Richard McDonald in San Bernardino, California. They bought appliances for their small hamburger restaurant from salesman Ray Kroc, who was intrigued by their need for eight malt and shake mixers. When Kroc visited the brothers in 1954 to see how a small shop could sell so many milk shakes, he discovered a simple, efficient format that permitted the brothers to produce huge quantities of food at low prices. A basic hamburger cost 15 cents, about half the price charged by competing restaurants. The self-service counter eliminated the need for waiters and waitresses; customers received their food quickly because hamburgers were cooked ahead of time, wrapped, and warmed under heat lamps.

Seeing great promise in their restaurant concept, Kroc offered to begin a franchise program for the McDonald brothers. On April 15, 1955, he opened the first McDonald's franchise in Des Plaines, Illinois, and in the same year launched the McDonald's Corporation, eventually buying out the McDonald brothers in 1961. The number of McDonald's outlets would top 1,000 before the end of the decade. Boosted by steady growth, the company's stock began trading publicly in 1965.

The public face of McDonald's was created in 1963 with the introduction of a clown named Ronald McDonald, while the double-arch "m" symbol became McDonald's most enduring logo in 1962, lasting far longer than the tall yellow arches that had once dominated the earlier restaurant rooftops. Other products and symbols would define the McDonald's brand, including the Big Mac (1968), the Egg McMuffin (1973), Happy Meals (1979), and Chicken McNuggets (1983).

In the late 1970's began "Burger Wars". Other fast food chains, like Burger King and Wendy's, began spreading seeing their place in the market. They all maintained aggressive advertising campaigns and low prices to try and stay competitive but McDonald's survived. They introduced McChicken, a chicken sandwich, in 1980 and Chicken McNuggets (after McChicken flopped) in 1983. Experts of that time thought that fast-food industry was saturated but McDonald's continued its growth. They opened their 10,000th restaurant in April 1988. By the beginning of the '90s they had more than 3,600 outlets in 58 countries not counting those in United States (where they had some 9,000). But 1990s brought difficulties. Too many experiments flopped and advertising campaigns failed. McDonald's had so many outlets that new started taking costumers from the old ones. Because of all that expansion in United States slowed down but McDonald's managed to get out of the problem by introducing popular toys with meals (Teenie Beanie Babies and toys from Disney and Pixar movies). In 1998, company had the first decrease in net income since the 1965 when it went public and resulted in job cuts.

Beginning of 2000s brought more job cuts along with lawsuits and accusations of selling unhealthy food. McDonald's restaurants were attacked around the world as symbols of globalization. Because of all of that McDonald's concentrated on improving the image and started selling more healthy food. Today, McDonald's is present in 119 countries where it has more than 35,000 restaurants and where more than 68 million customers are served daily.

McDonald's Corporation is the world's largest chain of hamburger fast food restaurants, serving more than 58 million customers daily.

The Hamburger Stand And How Ray Kroc Joined The Company

Customers line up outside the first McDonald's hamburger stand which was opened in 1948 by brothers Dick and Maurice McDonald in San Bernadino, Calif.

McDonald's had humble beginnings.

What is now the biggest fast food chain in the world began as a small hamburger stand in San Bernardino, Calif. Two brothers, Dick and Maurice "Mac" McDonald, opened the stand in 1940 as "McDonald's Bar-B-Q."

They later shut it down and reopened it in 1948, with a pared-down menu of just nine items, including hamburgers (15 cents) cheeseburgers (19 cents) and drinks, such as coffee, Coca-Cola, and Orangeade, for 10 cents.

In 1954, the stand caught the attention of Ray Kroc, an Illinois businessman who sold milkshake mixers.

Kroc had received a "huge" order of eight mixers from the brothers and he was intrigued, according to McDonald's. Kroc went to California to check out the business and "was stunned by the effectiveness of their operation."

Kroc convinced the brothers to give him franchise rights to their business, which he acquired in 1955. He opened the first McDonald's franchise, pictured below, in 1955 in Des Plaines, Ill.

The restaurant's sales on its first day totaled $366, according to the company.

By 1958, McDonald's had sold 100 million hamburgers and two years later, Kroc bought exclusive rights to the McDonald's. The company began rapidly building new restaurants and in 1965, there were 700 McDonald's restaurants throughout the U.S.

Now the biggest fast food chain in the world, McDonald's serves 70 million customers every day with sales topping $28 billion last year.

MCDONALD'S PRODUCT MIX

When the Dick and Mac McDonald opened their first restaurant in San Bernardino, California in 1948, they never could have imagined the extraordinary growth their company would experience. From modest beginnings, they found a winning formula selling high quality products quickly and low-cost. It was not until 1955 when Ray Kroc, a salesman from Chicago, became involved in the business that McDonald's really began to flourish. Kroc realized the same successful McDonald's formula could be exploited throughout the United States and beyond with the use of franchising. A franchise is an agreement or license to sell a company's products exclusively in a particular area, or to operate a business that carries that company's name.

In 1955, Kroc knew that the key to success was through rapid expansion; thus, the best way to achieve this was through offering franchises. Today, over 70 percent of McDonald's Restaurants are franchises. In 1986, the first franchised McDonald's opened in the United Kingdom. Now, there are over 1,150 restaurants, employing more than 49,000 people, of which 34 percent are operated by franchisees. Moreover, there are over 30,000 these restaurants in more than 119 countries, serving over 47 million customers around the world. In 2000 alone, McDonald's served over 16 billion customers. For perspective, that number is equivalent to providing a lunch and dinner for every man, woman, and child in the world! McDonald's global sales were over $40 billion, making it by far the largest food service company in the world.

Because of the invention of franchising and the development of some of the most creative marketing and branding campaigns, McDonald's is one of the world's most well-known, valuable brands holding a leading share in the globally branded, quick service restaurant segment of the informal dining-out market in virtually every country in which they do business. As a leader in the fast food industry, McDonald's is often targeted. Some of the ways McDonald's handles the attacks of the media and competition is by creating a marketing mix to highlight the positive impacts the organization. McDonald's must keep the strategic nature of its marketing efforts to stay on top and provide what customers want.

McDonald's menu includes hamburgers and cheeseburgers, the Big Mac, Quarter Pounder with Cheese, and Filet-O-Fish, several chicken sandwiches, Chicken

McNuggets, Snack Wraps, French fries, salads, oatmeal, shakes, McFlurry desserts, sundaes, soft-serve cones, pies, soft drinks, coffee, McCafé beverages, and other beverages. Also, the restaurants sell a variety of other products during limited-time promotions. The company offers the McRib sandwich on a seasonal basis, which adds to the company's appeal.

McDonald's restaurants in the U.S. and many international markets offer a full or limited breakfast menu. Breakfast offerings may include the Egg McMuffin or Sausage McMuffin with Egg, McGriddles, biscuit and bagel sandwiches, and hotcakes.

Unique international menu items

In Asia, many McDonald's branded restaurants also serve soups. In India, lamb often replaces beef in burgers due to the religious prohibition of beef consumption. In Indonesia and Singapore, menu items include McRice and Ebi (prawn or shrimp). In Germany and Western Europe, McDonald's serves higher-margin products like beer. In New Zealand, the company's restaurants serve a local favorite, meat pies!

The company sells over 75 hamburgers a second.

McDonald's claims that it has a sustainable supply chain in which it focuses on the three E's: ethics, environment, and economics. However, the company's focus is probably in the reverse order. Its supply chain is a complex web of direct and indirect suppliers that are held to clear standards for quality and efficiency. Indirect suppliers operate facilities such as grain mills and abattoirs. Farms and ranches raise cattle or grow wheat, lettuce, and other essential ingredients. Distribution centers coordinate purchasing and distribution to restaurants. Finally, processing facilities produce finished products like beverages, buns, and meat patties.

Companies that McDonald's has worked with in the past include Cargill, Smithfield Foods, Mullins Food Products, Bama Companies, Florette Agricola-Pentaflor, Aria Foods, Golden Foods, JBS, BRF, Kraft, Pepsico, Coca Cola, Tyson, and Griffith Laboratories.

Product in the Marketing mix of McDonalds

McDonald's places considerable emphasis on developing a menu which customers want. Market research establishes exactly what this is. However, customers' requirements change over time. In order to meet these changes, McDonald's has introduced new products and phased out old ones, and will continue to do so.

Care is taken not to adversely affect the sales of one choice by introducing a new choice, which will cannibalize sales from the existing one (trade off). McDonald's knows that items on its menu will vary in popularity.

Their ability to generate profits will vary at different points in their cycle. In India McDonalds has a diversified product range focusing more on the vegetarian products as most consumers in India are primarily vegetarian. The happy meal for the children is a great seller among others.

Marketing mix must focus on the product, pricing, promotion, and placement of item in order to make it successful. Marketing strategies must feature customer orientation, input, and accessibility in the fight to the top of the market. McDonald's is no different. One can recognize that McDonald's primary target market is children ages 3-11 and their parents. McDonald's understood that the parent was making the purchasing decision, most likely based on price.

Price in the Marketing mix of McDonalds

The customer's perception of value is an important determinant of the price charged. Customers draw their own mental picture of what a product is worth. A product is more than a physical item, it also has psychological connotations for the customer. The danger of using low price as a marketing tool is that the customer may feel that quality is being compromised. It is important when deciding on price to be fully aware of the brand and its integrity.

In India McDonalds classifies its products into 2 categories namely the branded affordability (BA) and branded core value products (BCV). The BCV products mainly include the McVeggie and McChicken burgers and the BA products include McAloo tikki and Chicken McGrill burgers. This has been done to satisfy consumers which different price perceptions.

Promotions in the Marketing mix of McDonalds

The promotions aspect of the marketing mix covers all types of marketing communications One of the methods employed is advertising, Advertising is conducted on TV, radio, in cinema, online, using poster sites and in the press for example in newspapers and magazines.

Other promotional methods include sales promotions, point of sale display, merchandising, direct mail, loyalty schemes, door drops, etc. The skill in marketing communications is to develop a campaign which uses several of these methods in a way that provides the most effective results.

For example, TV advertising makes people aware of a food item and press advertising provides more detail. Hence, McDonalds uses many above the line marketing methods. This may be supported by in-store promotions to get people to try the product and a collectable promotional device to encourage them to keep on buying the item.

At McDonalds the prime focus is on targeting children. In happy meals too which are targeted at children small toys are given along with the meal. Apart from this, various schemes for winning prices by way of lucky draws and scratch cards are given when an order is placed on the various meal combos.

Place in the Marketing mix of McDonalds

Place, as an element of the marketing mix, is not just about the physical location or distribution points for products. It encompasses the management of a range of processes involved in bringing products to the end consumer. McDonald's outlets are very evenly spread throughout the cities making them very accessible. Drive in and drive through options make McDonald's products further convenient to the consumers.

People in the Marketing mix of McDonalds

The employees in Mc Donald's have a standard uniform and Mc Donald's specially focuses on friendly and prompt service to its customers from their employees. All new franchises are trained in customer management and in keeping the customers happy.

They are also trained for handling negative responses from customers and what to do when there is high pressure on the outlet. Such kind of training is especially useful when the employee has no job experience and is working in a McDonald's outlet which is bound to get crowded on weekends or festivals.

Process in the Marketing mix if McDonalds

The food manufacturing process at Mc Donald's is completely transparent i.e. the whole process is visible to the customers. In fact, the fast food joint allows its customers to view and judge the hygienic standards at Mc Donald's. The customers are invited to check the ingredients used in food.

Physical evidence in the Marketing mix of McDonalds

McDonalds focuses on clean and hygienic interiors of is outlets and at the same time the exteriors are attractive and the fast food joint maintains a proper decorum at its joints.

The year in which some McDonald's Favorites were Introduced are:-

1955 – Hamburgers, cheeseburgers, fries, shakes, soft drinks, coffee and milk

1963 -Filet-O-Fish

1968 -Big Mac and Hot Apple Pie

1973 -Quarter Pounder and Egg McMuffin

1974 -McDonaldland Cookies

1977 -Breakfast Menu

1978 -Sundaes

1979 -Happy Meals

1983 -Chicken McNuggets

1986 -Biscuit Sandwiches

1987 -Salads

1998 -McFlurry Desserts

1999 -Breakfast Bagels

2000 -Chicken McGrill and Crispy Chicken

2001 -Big N' Tasty

2003 -Premium Salads, Newman's Own® salad dressings and McGriddles

2004 – Chicken Selects® Premium Breast Strips

McDonald's restaurants have a variety of strategies that apply to product, placement, promotion, and price that makes them one of the most successful, well-recognized organizations in the world.

MCDONALD'S CROSS-SELLING

Cross-selling is a technique that entices a customer to supplement his or her initial purchase with products that complement it.

Good cross-selling is an art. It is all about timing and relevance. It is in no way about manipulating customers. The most effective way to sell more to someone is when they have a genuine interest in it anyway.

And the textbook example is the McDonald's company's " would you like fries with that?". That small question allows McDonalds to sell over 4 million kilograms of fries globally every day. *

McDonalds' employees then ask every customer if they would like a drink or larger sizes. The incremental revenues due to these small cross and up sells do wonders to boost the company's bottom line. 69 million customers per day, being asked to buy more. Interesting, isn't it.

MCDONALD'S UP-SELLING

Upselling is a popular sales strategy in many industries. Upselling encourages a customer to purchase a more expensive model in the same product family, or to augment the original model with additional features.

"Would you like fries with that?" the McDonald's employee asks as you complete your Big Mac purchase. But this is not just a friendly reminder. This iconic question is an example of upselling: an intelligent technique for increasing sales on all channels.

McDonald's uses the purchase of a relatively cheap Big Mac as a lead generator. They know that once a customer is already at check out, they are more likely to add an additional item to their purchase. McDonald's recognizes that existing customers are an important source of lead generation.

MCDONALD'S CORPORATE REALITY

COUNTRIES WITH MCDONALD'S

McDonald's was founded in 1940 by brothers Richard and Maurice McDonald. It was originally intended to be a barbecue restaurant. At present, McDonald's is the second largest chain of fast food restaurants in the world, only after the casual sandwich chain Subway. It has an estimated 36,889 outlets across 120 countries. Around 68 million consumers are served a daily basis. The global headquarters of McDonald's are based in Oak Brook, Illinois, but there is a confirmation that it will be moved to Chicago in early 2018.

Since opening in California in the 1950s, McDonald's has expanded considerably throughout the world. At present, McDonald's operates 36,899 restaurants, 5,669 of which are company-owned and 31,230 of which are franchised. Its total property owned is said to have a value between 16 and 18 billion dollars.

Countries With McDonald's Restaurant

1. The United States - 14,146 locations

While some sources claim that there are closer to 16,000 McDonald's outlets in the United States, the official figure is a little lower at 14,146. The most McDonald's locations can be found in states with the largest populations, such as New York, California, and Texas, but the states with the highest concentration of restaurants are Ohio, Michigan, Kansas, Maryland, and Louisiana.

Only around 31% of McDonald's revenue comes from the United States, which is less than from Europe overall. Additionally, McDonald's has more locations than any other fast food restaurant in Europe, but this is not the case in the United States, where the location leader is sandwich giant Subway.

2. Japan - around 2,975 locations

McDonald's first and most important Asian marketplace is Japan, where there were nearly 3,000 locations as of 2018. This is a shrinking or consolidating market, as there were 3,700 open McDonald's restaurants in Japan during 2007. In 2015, the company was closing a location in Japan on average every three days. Store closings continued as McDonald's struggled with higher input costs and a health-conscious consumer base, but the trend seems to be slowing.

3. China - around 2,700 locations

While the golden arches reached Japan in 1971, Hong Kong in 1975 and the Philippines in 1981, China did not allow McDonald's until 1990. Growth has been strong since, and now only Japan has more locations in Asia. Japan and China combine for roughly 20% of McDonald's total gross revenue. In a highly publicized release, McDonald's said in late 2017 that they plan to nearly double their Chinese outlets.

4. Germany - 1,480 locations

Germany has the largest McDonald's presence in Europe, operating almost 1,500 outlets across the country. Given the German propensity toward speed and convenience, it is no wonder the fast food model of McDonald's has thrived in an otherwise very healthy-conscious country.

5. Canada - 1,450 locations

Canada technically has more McDonald's than every European nation outside of Germany. The first Canadian McDonald's opened in Richmond, British Columbia, in June 1967. Canada may be nuzzling the United States, but it looks like the massive country isn't taking the same approach to cuisine, having less than one-tenth the locations of its Southern neighbor.

6. France - 1,419 locations

The densely populated country, well known for its fine dining, has embraced the novelty of McDonald's. In 2017, France was the second largest European market for the hamburger chain.

7. The United Kingdom - 1,274 locations

The Eurozone loves McDonald's. This region boasts the restaurant chain's greatest amount of revenue, as well as its highest margins. In fact, McDonald's is the largest fast-food chain in virtually every European nation, with odd exceptions such as Iceland, which banned McDonald's to protect local restaurants. Together, Germany, France, and the United Kingdom account for more than half of the European McDonald's. It is doubtful that Brexit will affect this specific consumer habit.

8. Australia - 920 locations

McDonald's in Australia remains a highly profitable market, crossing over the $4 billion sales mark year after year. For a country so sparsely populated, they have developed a McDonald's habit that is a steady revenue producer for the company.

9. Brazil - 812 locations

The largest South American market for McDonald's is found in Brazil, which is home to over 800 locations. Brazil's government opened an investigation into McDonald's in March 2016 after complaints from unionized labor, regarding franchise owners. This fizzled out, and Brazil remains a strong satellite outpost for McDonald's.

10. Russia - 649 locations

McDonald's managed to get into the Soviet Union just as the Iron Curtain was crumbling in 1990. It now operates almost 650 restaurants in Russia, opening 45 during 2016.

Countries With No McDonald's Restaurant

Bermuda does not have any McDonald's due to a government ban on foreign restaurants. Bolivia currently has no McDonald's restaurant, after low sales forced its departure. McDonald's is absent from many countries across Africa, as well as Central Asia.

Is McDonald's the Largest Fast-Food Chain in the World?

McDonald's is a huge and mighty fast-food chain but is not the largest. Subway is the largest, with 43,985 stores in 112 countries as of early 2018. Again, many of these "countries" are not independent and are merely territories. And Subway's restaurant count certainly includes all those that are part of other buildings (as half of a convenience store, for example) rather than counting only standalone restaurant locations.

The third runner-up is KFC (formerly Kentucky Fried Chicken), with 20,500 locations in 125 countries, according to its official website. Other widely spread worldwide food brands that the United States has exported include Pizza Hut (14,000 locations, 120 countries), and Starbucks (24,000 locations, 75 markets).

A Symbol Of Globalization

McDonald's has become an emblem of globalization so much that the term "McDonaldization" has emerged. The Economist magazine uses the Big Mac Index, which compares the Big Mac's cost in different world currencies, which can be used to establish the purchasing power parity (PPP) of currencies.

BUSINESS STRATEGY OF MCDONALD'S

1. The Fast Food Concept

Fast food is a concept employed in restaurant operation that involves the mass production and preparation of ready-to-eat food products to accommodate a large number of customers and thus, increase sales volume, improve operational effectiveness and efficiency, and promote convenience by reducing waiting time.

Both Richard and Maurice introduced the "Speedee Service System" in 1948 that utilized and expanded further the fast food concept earlier practiced by the American hamburger chain White Castle. The system not only applies the concept of fast food but also the principles of production line manufacturing to prepare a range of food items quickly.

Today, the speedee service system and the general fast food concept remain central to the daily operations of every McDonald's branch. The company has applied these practices not only in its core restaurant business but also in other restaurant models such as the McDrive drive-in branches, McExpress food stalls, and the McCafè coffee shops.

2. Franchising Business Model

Central to the business strategy of McDonald's and one of the primary reasons it has successfully expanded across the United States and in different parts of the world is a business model based on franchising. The company began franchising in 1953. It further attracted franchisees after its acquisition by Ray Kroc in 1961.

The fast food concept and the overall operational efficiency observed in different branches have attracted the attention of investors and the restaurant industry. Since the 1960s, individuals and groups have always been eager to secure a franchise license to operate their own McDonald's branch because of the high return on their investments. Note that Kroc was initially a franchisee who opened his first branch in 1954 before taking over the company seven years after.

Based on the business model, McDonald's generates some its revenues from the rent, royalties, and fees paid by the franchisees although it also earns from the restaurants it directly owns and operates. Franchising has allowed the company to expand its market reach not only across the U.S. but also in developed and developing countries.

3. Joint Ventures With Other Organizations

Franchising is not the only business model of McDonald's. Another way it enters in and expands to specific geographic markets is through joint ventures with local business organizations and in some cases, governments or state-owned companies.

In 2017, the company has entered a joint venture with three Chinese companies: CITIC Ltd., CITIC Capital, and Carlyle Capital. This move was aimed at increasing the presence of restaurants across mainland China, increasing its global sales by digging deeper into the Chinese market and of course, increasing the number of its branches.

A joint venture enables an organization to enter a foreign market through access to local resources and the use of suitable management competencies, as well as localization of a global brand and the acculturation of the entire business. In the case of McDonald's, the joint venture with the Chinese companies will enable it to secure better locations for its branches and gain local market knowledge.

4. Real Estate Development and Ownership

It is interesting to note that more than just a fast food restaurant, McDonald's is also a developer and owner of real estate properties. The estimated collective value of these properties is around USD 18 billion to USD 30 billion.

Aside from collecting royalty and licensing fees from franchisees, the company also collects rents from these individual businesses. It essentially buys and develops real estate properties and have them leased to franchisees at a large markup value. McDonald's has developed and operated lands not only in the U.S. but also in other countries.

The strategy stems from Kroc. To be more specific, he hired Harry Sonneborn in 1956 who advised him that the real income would not be generated through franchising alone but also to the development and leasing of real estate. McDonald's currently charge franchisees either stipulated markups of about 40 percent of lease costs or 5 percent of the sales—whichever is higher.

5. Supply Chain Management

Supply chain management is another critical element of the business strategy of McDonald's. Remember that the company not only sells food products but also uses other resources for its daily operations to include kitchen equipment, dining provisions, and materials for its physical stores.

The company has been utilizing long-term contracts with suppliers to ensure a steady supply of the resources it needs. For example, the company has secured contracts with farm owners, as well as food and beverage producers in different parts of the world to supply them with products needed for the preparation of its specific fast food productions.

McDonald's has also subjected its suppliers under strict standards through performance management to promote quality across different branches in different parts of the world. Performance management ensures that branches are able to serve products that are consistent with the standards set forth by the company. It also drives suppliers to innovate to improve operational efficiency and promote further quality.

6. Marketing and Advertising

There are several key activities that form part of the overall marketing strategy of McDonald's. Note that it has obliged franchisees to observe its branding standards based on its trademarks to ensure consistency in branding and marketing messages. These standards are an essential part of the contracts with franchisees.

It has also invested heavily in advertising through traditional and digital media. Similar to The Coca-Cola Company, the company has seasonal advertising campaigns and regional ones that are tailor fitted to a particular occasion or event and culture of the geographic market.

Product strategy through localization is also an essential marketing consideration. The company has also developed food products based on the culture of the locality to address the preferences of consumers in specific geographic markets. This is the reason why menus in different McDonald's branches in different countries are varied. For example, in Japan, branches there offer food products demonstrating the fusion between American and Japanese cuisines.

How Much Is McDonald's Really Worth?

Fast-food pioneer McDonald's has long been the stalwart in its industry, transforming the nature of the restaurant business and creating a trend that has lasted for more than half a century. With more than 36,000 locations around the world, McDonald's has a global presence, and its golden arches are known the world over as an American icon.

At the same time, long-term investors have earned huge returns by owning McDonald's stock and holding it over the decades. Yet there are many methods for coming up with a corporate valuation, and many investors are curious whether McDonald's stock accurately reflects its actual worth. Below, we'll take a closer look at the net worth of McDonald's, using several different measures, to see whether the current share price is consistent with the fast-food giant's true value.

McDonald's currently has about 853 million shares outstanding. With a share price of around $117 per share, that puts McDonald's market capitalization at right around $100 billion.

Some investors don't like the fact that market capitalization doesn't take into account how much cash and debt a company has. Instead, they prefer enterprise value, which goes beyond those figures to drill down on the value of the actual business that produces profit for the company. When you account for McDonald's cash and debt, its enterprise value works out to more than $121 billion.

However, you get a much different picture when you look at McDonald's from an accountant's perspective. The company's balance sheet provides a different view of McDonald's, and it's one in which the fast-food company seems to be richly valued by the market.

McDonald's most recent financial statements put a value of $33.1 billion on its assets. That includes $3.1 billion in cash and short-term investments, another $1.3 billion in accounts receivable, and $600 million in inventory, prepaid expenses, and other current assets. In addition, McDonald's plants, property, and equipment make up almost $23 billion after taking accumulated depreciation into account. Long-term investments account for less than $1 billion, and adding in about $4 billion in goodwill and other long-term assets brings you to the total for the restaurant operator.

Against those assets, McDonald's has substantial liabilities. Debt amounts to $26 billion, all of which is long-term. Accounts payable and accrued expenses add another $2.4 billion, and taxes due and other liabilities amount to another $4 billion or so. All told, liabilities amount to $32.5 billion.

That leaves a scant $640 million in shareholder equity for McDonald's shares. That works out to a book value of just $0.75 per share, or less than 1% of the company's current share price. Trading at a premium to book value isn't all that unusual for a stock, but the extent of the premium here reflects a gradual deterioration in McDonald's book value in recent years.

For those who believe that investors are rational, it's easy to conclude that McDonald's true value clearly isn't reflected in its accounting statements. For instance, a huge part of McDonald's worth comes from its brand identity, and in its most recent annual survey of major global brands late last year, Interbrand ranked McDonald's No. 9. The report put a value of $39.8 billion on McDonald's brand identity, and even though that was down 6% from year-earlier levels, it still recognizes the lengths to which the fast-food giant has gone to produce a marketing message that puts its competitors to shame.

Ray Kroc Net Worth

Ray Kroc was an American businessman and entrepreneur who had a net worth of $600 million at the time of his death in 1984. That's the same as $1.4 billion after adjusting for inflation. Ray Kroc was born in Oak Park, Illinois in October 1902 and passed away in January 1984. He was best known for being responsible for the popularity of the McDonald's brand. Kroc joined McDonald's in 1954 and helped expand the franchise nationally and then globally. Later on his life he claimed to have founded the company although that is credited to the McDonald brothers. He was the owner of the Major League Baseball team San Diego Padres from 1974 until he passed away in 1984. Kroc was listed in the Time 100: The Most Important People of the Century list. He was portrayed by actor Michael Keaton in the film The Founder in 2016. Ray Kroc passed away on January 14, 1984 at 81 years old from heart failure and was married three times including to Joan Kroc. When Joan died in 2003, she was worth $3 billion. She gave nearly the entire fortune away to charity. At McDonald's current stock price, the Kroc's fortune would be worth $18 billion.

REAL ESTATE OR HAMBURGER

REITs can be excellent stocks to add to any long-term investment portfolio. Not only are REITs excellent income generators, but they have the potential to produce some impressive returns over time as property values rise. Investors can choose REITs that specialize in a wide variety of properties, such as apartments, offices, shopping malls, self-storage facilities, and more.

The fast food giant came from humble beginnings. The McDonald brothers, sons of Irish immigrants, first opened up a hot dog stand in 1937 in Pasadena before venturing out to open their first restaurant. By 1953 they had seen some success using an assembly line method of burger preparation. They'd already started franchising the system, but not the atmosphere or name of their restaurant.

Meanwhile, a milkshake machine salesman named Ray Kroc had taken notice of the brother's restaurant concept after selling them 8 of his machines. Ray could see the massive potential and quickly partnered with the McDonald brothers, serving as a franchising agent. After six years of working with the McDonalds and finding their ambition ultimately falling short of his own, he elected to buy them out and became the owner of McDonald's Corporation in 1961.

McDonald's logo Franchising is a model by which fast food chains can expand quickly and efficiently by using the money of small investors. Ray Kroc perfected new franchising techniques, increasing the corporation's size while maintaining strict control of its products. Around this time is when CFO Sonneborn came up with the strategy that McDonald's continues to use today.

Instead of making money by selling supplies to franchisees or demanding huge royalties...the McDonald's Corporation became the landlord to its franchisees.

They bought the properties and then leased them out – at large markups. In addition to that regular income, the corporation would take a percentage of each shop's gross sales.

Today McDonald's makes its money on real estate through two methods. Its real estate subsidiary will buy and sell hot properties while also collecting rents on each of its franchised locations. McDonald's restaurants are in over 100 countries and have probably served over 100 billion hamburgers. There are over 36,000 locations worldwide, of which only 15% are owned and operated by the McDonald's corporation directly. The rest are franchisee-operated.

During the 2008 recession, McDonald's leaned heavily on this facet of their business as they capitalized on an anemic property market – buying up more of the land and buildings where it operates. The company owns about 45% of the land and 70% of the buildings at their 36,000+ locations (the rest is leased).

It's a brilliant strategy. Being able to collect on rents helps insulate them from the ups and downs of the business of flippin' burgers. You have to make rent after all.

In 2014, the McDonald's corporation made $27.4 billion in revenues, of which fully $9.2 billion came from franchised locations and the rest ($18.2 billion) was from company-operated restaurants.

Hold up, we can hear you saying "The majority of their revenue came from company-operated restaurants, a full two-thirds!" Yep, but what about the profit margins?

It costs way more money to run your own store than it does to sit back and collect cash.

McDonald's keeps close to 82% of all their franchise-generated revenue versus only 16% of its company-operated restaurant revenue. So who's really contributing more to the bottom line?

Of that $18.2 billion generated by company-operated stores in 2014, the corporation keeps just $2.9 billion. Of the $9.2 billion coming from franchisees, the corporation keeps $7.6 billion.

In 2014 McDonald's made 4.75 billion dollars in net income (sweet profit dollars). Essentially we could say that 82% of every dollar in profit is generated by a franchisee. That's an intense statement about a "burger company".

It's because of the unique makeup of McDonald's (and the fact that the business is struggling on a whole) that investors are pressuring the company to spin off its land and buildings into a separate entity. Revenues in 2014 were down from year-ago levels and 2015 looks to be even more depressed than 2014 but if you considered just the real-estate portion of the business, McDonald's suddenly becomes way more exciting.

Imagine a company with $40 billion dollars' worth of real estate assets (before taking depreciation into account) and yearly revenues of $9 billion, of which nearly $4 billion is profit. That's the McDonald's real estate investment trust (REIT). Not bad right?

To put those numbers into further perspective, this fictional REIT would represent over 40% of McDonald's current market cap while bringing in 80% of its profits.

McDonald's is a great example of how diversification helps to not just grow a business's income but also lower its financial risks. McDonald's is both a fast food and real estate business. As a fast food company, it doesn't just operate its own restaurants, it also franchises the brand. By franchising the brand, they're able to achieve much larger economies of scale because other companies or entrepreneurs finance the expansion of the brand into many other places all over the world. They're also able to earn more income via higher margins since the income they earn from the percentage of sales of their franchisees don't require them to spend for operating those franchised branches.

Relying on income from franchises alone can be rather risky. Why? Franchise agreements aren't forever and as such, they can end. What happens if many franchisees terminate their agreement? However unlikely, it's still a business risk and by continuing to build and operate company owned branches, they are able to mitigate potential effects of such a risk.

Being in the real estate business also helps McDonald's earn more income and somewhat diversify its portfolio. Buying properties and leasing them to franchisees is a very clever way of effectively doubling the income earned from franchisees! And for the other properties they don't lease out to franchisees, they can always rent them to someone else or simply flip them for a profit.

They may, however, need to come up with new ways to keep in step with their industry's current developments if this diversified portfolio is to continue being profitable.

McDonald's has been struggling for a while now to compete against fast-casual joints like Chipotle and Shake Shack. They used to hold the promise of good fast-food but now the food is neither fast, nor good. In fact, in 2014, the average drive-thru wait time was over three minutes (the longest it has ever been in about 15 years).

The rot has started to set in, and unless the company pivots quickly and efficiently…they might see themselves left behind. Consumer's tastes have changed and unless McDonald's proves itself agile enough to adapt with the times, you might see the company get cannibalized for some time yet.

The success of McDonald's can be attributed in part to the taste of the iconic fast food chain's shakes and burgers. But the real secret sauce has everything to do with how the company has quietly become more a real estate company than a restaurant chain.

About 85% of the company in 2016 was represented by franchisee-run locations—people who agree to operate individual McDonald's restaurants with a licensed privilege to the branding. But rather than collect a lot in royalties or sell its franchisees cooking equipment, McDonald's makes much of its revenue by buying the physical properties and then leasing them to franchisees, often at large mark-ups.

The company keeps about 82% of the revenue generated by franchisees, compared with only about 16% of the revenue from its company-operated locations, which is reduced by the expenses of running those operations, according to the investment blog Wall Street Survivor.

In a 2015 analysis of McDonald's franchising, Business week cited estimates by Janney Capital Markets. The total sales for an average location clocked in at $2.7 million per store each year, with $1.7 million in gross profits after accounting for food and paper costs. But then there are also other expenses: rent, payroll, advertising, promotions, operating supplies, insurance, and more. Average operating income after accounting for all those expenses rounded out to a take-home of just $154,000 per year for a single franchisee.

The average rent per store amounts to about 22% of average gross profits each year for franchisees. The company has more than 36,000 locations across more than 100 countries, so that adds up quickly. Better put, McDonald's has more than $30 billion in real estate assets, and annual profits that float around $4.5 billion, according to company financial disclosures.

The number of franchisee McDonald's locations has been steadily growing, as the company-owned number has dropped slightly in the last decade.

The emphasis on real estate may also pay off for the company at tax time. The US tax code includes several provisions favorable to real estate investors and landlords (which US president Donald Trump also appears to have benefited from).

Consider depreciation. Some types of property—such as cars—lose value over time, so it makes sense to offer tax breaks for their lost value. Real estate, on the other hand, often increases in value over time, and yet the IRS allows owners to deduct depreciation from taxable rent. This is something that McDonald's can very easily take advantage of, says Xian Sun, a professor of corporate finance at Johns Hopkins University. McDonald's reported $1.39 billion in depreciation in 2016, but it's unclear what portion of that was depreciation of real estate rented to franchisees. The company did not immediately respond to a request for comment.

Additionally, in the last two decades real estate values have increased, which means the overall collateral value of the company's property has increased, too. So when McDonald's wants to borrow money to make new investments, it can do so at relatively cheap rates.

The value of all that real estate also provides a lot of insulation when the company needs to weather fluctuations in the larger burger business, as consumer habits and larger economic headwinds shift. McDonald's CEO, Steve Easterbrook, is being paid handsomely—more than $15 million a year—to navigate the company through what's becoming a rough patch, in which sales have shrunk in the face of a more competitive market for three years in a row.

McDonald's has been making all sorts of changes in the last year to try and keep up with fast casual brands such as Chipotle, Panera Bread Company, and others. It's about to roll out a mobile ordering platform; it began offering all-day breakfast and it recently announced it will be using fresh beef patties across the US for some of its burgers.

MCDONALD'S FRANCHISING

McDonald's has a unique franchise model that empowers local entrepreneurs.

McDonald's restaurants can be found in more than 100 countries around the globe. More than 90% of our restaurants worldwide are owned and operated by independent Franchisees.

A grant of a McDonald's franchise authorizes franchisees to operate a McDonald's restaurant business at a specific location and to use the McDonald's System in the operation of that restaurant business for a specific period of time. The franchisor offers four types of franchises:

Traditional Restaurant: franchise offered is located in freestanding buildings, store fronts, food courts, and other locations. The franchisee operates a full-menu restaurant, offering the public a high standard of quality and uniformity in food and service.

Satellite Locations: The franchisee is granted the right to operate the franchise in a retail store, strip center, airport, universities, hospitals, and other diverse locations. These restaurants serve a scaled-down menu of a traditional McDonald's Restaurant and in some cases may also serve non-McDonald's trademarked products.

STO and STR Locations: 'Small Town Oil' locations are situated in fuel stations/convenience stores, and operate a full-menu McDonald's restaurant within the shared space. 'Small Town Retail' locations that anchor a small retail center in rural communities.

BFL Franchises: 'Business Facilities Lease' franchises grant franchises with leases that include the business facilities.

Training Overview: The franchisor operates Hamburger University (HU), the international training center for the McDonald's System. The content and duration of all operations courses, which are offered at HU and various local sites, are revised and reconsidered from time to time to meet the needs of the franchisees. All courses and learning events are offered at frequent intervals and are designed to give franchisees specific skill sets in the various facets of the conduct of a McDonald's restaurant. The basic minimum core training, which franchisees must complete to be qualified to operate a McDonald's restaurant, is known as the Restaurant Leadership curriculum. Restaurant Leadership curriculum is deployed through Campus and Fred, which allows franchisees to complete and track the progress of their assigned learning online. It takes approximately two years to complete all learning plans, from Shift Manager through General Manager. The complete training program and materials include many elements. As part of the training program, franchisees must perform and master all of the crew and management functions at the restaurant. At the opening of the restaurant, a franchise business partner will spend time with franchisees providing assistance and refinement of previous training and instruction. Franchisees must complete the training program successfully before signing the Franchise Agreement or paying any money to the franchisor. There are no further mandatory training requirements for franchisees beyond the Restaurant Leadership curriculum. However, annual meetings, conventions, various workshops, and other training sessions may be conducted on an ongoing basis within each field office, and McDonald's may require franchisees to pay for the costs associated with that ongoing training or participation. Additionally, optional courses may be offered to franchisees or their employees for a fee.

Territory Granted: McDonald's franchises contain a limited grant of authority to use the McDonald's System in the operation of the specific restaurant developed by McDonald's at that address. Franchisees will not receive an exclusive territory. Franchisees may face competition from other franchisees, from outlets that the franchisor owns, or from other channels of distribution or competitive brands that the franchisor controls. The Franchise Agreement does not contain any exclusive grant, exclusive area, exclusive territorial rights, protected territory, or any right to exclude, control, or impose conditions on the location or development of future McDonald's restaurants at any time.

Obligations and Restrictions: Franchisees are required to provide full time and best efforts to and personal on-premises supervision of, the day-to-day operation of their McDonald's restaurant business. Franchisees may sell only products authorized by McDonald's and use the premises only as a McDonald's restaurant. In the dispensing and sale of these products, franchisees may use only packaging, paper goods, ingredients, and handling and preparation methods that meet the McDonald's System specifications and quality standards which the franchisor may designate and modify.

Term of Agreement and Renewal: The length of the initial traditional franchise term is generally 20 years. The Satellite term varies, and the length of the franchise term for STO and STR locations are generally 10 years. BFL term length is generally three years. Franchisees are given no right to renew or extend the franchise after the term of the contract. A Rewrite (New Term) Policy is not part of the previous Franchise Agreement.

Financial Assistance: Typically, no financing arrangements are offered by the franchisor. The franchisor issues an Operator's Lease for each site owned or leased by McDonald's. The Operator's Lease is a standard commercial lease under which the franchisee pays rent to the franchisor for use of the premises. The Operator's Lease does not contain any financing terms. For BFL franchises, the Operator's Lease provides for the lease of the restaurant's business facilities as well as the premises. The franchisor's predecessor may, at its discretion, guarantee loans made by a third party lender, Bank of America, N.A., a National Banking Association, to franchisees for remodeling existing restaurants, working capital, delinquent accounts receivable, refinancing existing restaurant loans, acquiring restaurant businesses from McOpCo companies, purchasing restaurant assets by exercising the option under a BFL Rider, and for other reasons approved by McDonald's.

McDonald's Franchises

McDonald's is known around the world for its burgers, fries and shakes. Its huge worldwide success and recognition ensure a McDonald's franchise is a strong candidate to make money. Most franchisees buy existing restaurants from the corporation or from other McDonald's owner/operators. Only a few purchase and build on a new site. As of 2011, 87 percent of McDonald's franchisees own more than one restaurant. All current franchisees are owner/operators; the company does not permit absentee ownership of its franchises. When considering a site, be aware that McDonald's usually will give preference to a proven franchisee over a new one when awarding select, demonstrably successful sites.

Location Requirements

The location of each unit is a major element of its potential success. For that reason, the company keeps a close watch on where its stores can be located. The ideal site for a stand-alone restaurant will be 50,000 square feet, although units have been developed on both smaller and larger sites. A corner location with the option to put up signs visible from two major streets is considered optimal, as is a site near a major intersection with traffic signals. Ample parking space is required and must meet all applicable local parking codes. Size and space requirements are adapted for mall, airport and some downtown locations.

Facility Considerations

Your McDonald's location will have to meet stringent inspections to ensure its food preparation, storage and counter areas are safe, clean and sufficiently large to meet client demand. The seating area is subject to safety and health inspections, and will be reviewed in terms of traffic flow and maximum capacity. Each location is required to have restroom facilities for males and females. Drive-through locations must meet local traffic and safety requirements, including clear markings for drive-through lanes and vehicle size restrictions. Additional space is required for restaurants at which the franchisee wants to have a McDonald's Play Place. Space requirements vary depending on whether the play area is inside or outdoors.

Financial Requirements

Because of its international name recognition and record of success, purchasing a McDonald's franchise requires a major financial commitment. The franchise fee alone is $45,000, with the total investment required ranging between $1 million and $2 million, according to Entrepreneur Magazine. The term of the franchise agreement is typically 20 years, at which time it can be renewed. McDonald's requires potential investors to demonstrate a minimum of $500,000 in non-borrowed liquid assets to even be considered for a franchise. The down payment is typically 25 percent of the total cost to purchase an existing restaurant and 40 percent for a new restaurant. Other fees include annual service fees and rental costs.

MCDONALD'S LAYOUT, PROCESS TYPE AND USE OF TECHNOLOGIES

The strategy refers to the overall working and general environment offered by the McDonald.

It includes the personal level, service and product layout, interior and exterior.

McDonald has a policy to serve the fresh food to its customers in a minimum time and at the same time they want to get as many as possible customers to get the more income. The most important thing on which McDonald operational department concentrate is the customer's satisfaction. Customers satisfaction can only be achieved if it serves the customers with a good quality food in a quickly with minimum price. In order to perform this whole process McDonald has a very specific type of layout. This layout gives an easy access to the staff to serves the customers in a quick way. At the till when a staff serves the customer, staff has a everything in its reach required by the customer.

McDonald keep maximum number of tills opens to serves the customers and each staff takes average one minute to serves the customer. The chairs are arranged in such a way that it gives a minimum disruption to the people who are standing in the queue.

In the kitchen department McDonald has selected high efficiency fryers which take minimum time to fry the chips. Operations manager has assigned the task to different staff members according to their ability.

McDonald get most of the things in ready to serve form from its main headquarter which decrease the cost of producing the food and it also help the McDonald to keep the quality same all over its stores. Staff in McDonald only has to put the food in oil and it gets ready to serve. It also helps the McDonald to save lot of storage cost.

In order to keep the system runs smoothly McDonald always keeps good relation with the suppliers. Their supplier makes sure that they deliver the goods to McDonald in the minimum possible time. (Swearingen, 2003)

STRATEGIC IMPORTANCE OF LAYOUT

Proper layout enables:

It makes the utilization of space, equipment and people more efficient.

It enables the movements of information, materials and peoples more effective.

It boosts the employee morale and helps to provide him safer working conditions.

It helps to improve the customer's relations with clients.

Flexibility

Layout design mean the overall working and general environment offered by the McDonald. It includes the personal level, service and product layout, interior and exterior etc.

STRATEGIES:

Exterior

McDonald sets its premises in proper manner to handle any number of customers easily. The building design is standard worldwide but it may be have some difference in size or in exterior according to the location. It enables them to save time, satisfy their customers, comfortable environment for both employees and customers. Ray Kroc was the first person in McDonald's history who took the initiative to franchise the McDonald. He also maintain the McDonald outlooks, its signs and layout same everywhere in the world which has directly improved the sale of the company. As it has an attractive layout and eye catching sign boards.

Interior:

Interiors are set to be "depoliticized." In addition to new restaurant lighting, menu boards, artwork and graphics, new materials will offer choice when it comes to decor selection. Technology perks include Wi-Fi, programmed music, and video.

MCDONALD'S USE OF TECHNOLOGIES

McDonalds has invested a huge amount of money on creating a technology board which has help the McDonald to adopt new and new technologies in its operations with time. The main job of this board is to recommend the management to buy those kind of equipment which are very effective in saving the energy as well as are more productive.

In 2001 McDonald has start investing money in the improvements of point to sale ordering system and at the same time linking the point to sale system with the back office computer in all over the world. So this thing has helped the management to know what actually happening inside the business. What customer likes and what they dislikes.

McDonald has invested capital in the improvement of electronic payment system as well which has make possible to process the transactions in less than 4 seconds.

McDonald uses the best equipment to carry out the day to day operation in its outlet.

MCDONALD EXPLOTATION OF VALUE CHAIN AND QUALITY

PORTER'S FIVE FORCES ANALYSIS

Competition

Restaurant industry is highly competitive industry. There are many small fast food businesses in the industry that fight each other to improve their customer base. McDonald is not exception to this. Since its establishment in 1940, MCD has excelled in this sector. Nevertheless to stay in the competition, it started with MCafe. This helped the company to stay in the business as a major fast food business. Another major step came out when McDonald started breakfast to compete with the existing businesses serving breakfast. Hence this industry is extremely competitive and the MDC should be up to date with customer taste and preferences. Quality is very important for McDonald in order to stay in the market but at the same time it has to keep the prices minimum to maintain the cost leadership.

Get help with your essay today, from our professional essay writers!

Qualified writers in the subject of international business are ready and waiting to help you with your studies.

Get help with your essay

View professionally written samples

Ease of entry

Although it is hard to enter in the restaurant business as it demand a lot of investment and it is hard to establish a distinct brand name as well. There is a cost of entry in the market and there is high research and development cost. Large established companies like McDonald perform compose it more easier said than done to enter and achieve something within the souk, new entrant find with the intention of they are facade with worth antagonism from offered string eating place. At the same McDonald working hard to maintain the quality same throughout the time. It is aware that if it compromise on its quality then it will make very much easier for the new entrant to attract the customers with better quality of its food products.

Substitutes

McDonald keeps a very close watch on its quality because it is aware that customers have many others substitutes of its food products. e.g. MDC burgers, Beverages and dairy products.

Strength of Suppliers

The supplier's power in the fast food manufacturing is quite miniature unless the foremost feature of the item for consumption is not voluntarily on hand.

Strength of Buyers

Relatively strength of buyers in this industry is relatively low.

PORTER'S FIVE FORCES ANALYSIS OF VALUE CHAIN

The main objectives of these kinds of activities are to give the customer a level of value which is more than the cost of activities. This has enables the McDonald to gain more profits.

The primary value chain activities are:

Inbound Logistics

Inbound logistics is the raw material McDonald received in its warehouse and then distribute it to different branches according to their requirements McDonald has an efficient warehousing and transporting goods to its branches. All the products are made in the warehousing and goods are distributed as per the requirement of each branch.

Operations

It is the activities which are being conducted in order to transform the inputs into finished products and services. McDonald has a very good operation system as it has trained staff for each task in the kitchen. Most of its product is already in the ready to serve form. All they have to put them in the ovens or in the oil and the product get ready to serve in the minimum possible time which normally takes from 1-5 minutes.

Outbound Logistics

Outbound logistics mean to keep the finished goods in warehouses and then distribute them to different branches. McDonald has a very well established transporting system. As all of its products are prepared at the warehouse, so in order to improve the distribution process it has applied the IT technology which inform the warehouse body that which branch is running out of the products, so before the products get finished it immediately make available the product to the branch. This process is very cost effective as branches do not need to have the stock room for the goods.

Marketing & Sale

It is a complete science that McDonald use to market its products in order to generate more sales.

Service

All the extra activities which are provided to customers even after the sale of goods.

The primary activities are supported by :

Technology development

Technologies helps the McDonald to access the activities done inside the business which are as follow:

Cost advantage

Keep a eye on the costs and minimizing it out of the value adding actions.

According to the porter's five forces analysis McDonald competes with the forces which are inside the business in order to gain the maximum profitability. So it proves that business profitability is took place in the porter's five forces mode.

Further there are Secondary support activities which directly supporting the operational activities of the business. HRM department make it possible for the business to get the energetic people to perform the operations. They always keep motivating the staff to work hard. The Management makes possible to select the technology which is cost effective together with the efficiency.

McDonald is a very well established organization. The success of the McDonald is completely based on the extensive research of the market internal and external forces. It has done research on the people behavior of specific country, on their culture, buying power and social issue. McDonald has paid special attention on the location of the business, its interior and exterior outlook and types of technologies it going to use to get the maximum production at short time. The most important thing which it focused on was the quality and the market forces which directly affect the business.

LEADERSHIP OF RAY KROC

Ray Kroc is the man behind the multimillion dollar fast food empire, MacDonald's.

In his life, he has built the fast food chain from a simple hamburger restaurant to a multi-billion dollar franchise that has reached almost every part of the world today.

Ray Kroc was born in 1902 in the city of Illinois. He had grown up to be a brash, enthusiastic young man who was a visionary and a salesman.

During World War I, although he was underage, he still signed up to be trained as a ambulance driver, but he never made to the front lines as the war ended before his training did.

After the war, he worked in many professions as a paper cup salesman, a pianist, a musician as well as at the Chicago Radio Station.

His breakthrough came with his fascination with the multi-mixers. He saw the potential in the McDonald's brothers' hamburger restaurant in churning out burgers after burgers like clockwork.

He suggested expansion to the brothers and volunteered to be the person to expand the restaurant chain. He saw great potential in the concept that the brothers did not.

Eventually he would buy over the restaurant from the brothers at $2.7 million. Ray Kroc would revolutionize the dining industry by created an assembly line method of selling his burgers that would be standardized throughout the world.

By 1963, McDonald's would have sold its 1 billionth burger and open its 500th restaurant.

At the end of his life in 1984, Ray Kroc amassed a personal fortune of $500 million, and in 2007, the McDonald's Corporation that he founded had achieved a revenue of $22 billion.

Awards and Honors

These are some awards that Ray Kroc has been noted for:

The Ray Kroc Award, an award given to Macdonald's top 1% managers, is named after him.

Visionary

While he was convincing the McDonald brothers of his plan, his mind began to visualize the thousands of McDonald stores in every city all over America. At first, he was excited by the idea of these stores having his multi-mixers in each of them. He was then in the business of selling those machines that turn out milk-shakes.

Like any good leader, Ray held by his vision and persuaded others to embrace that vision.

Committed

During his days as a paper cup salesman, Ray was committed to following rules and principles that made him a good salesman and later, as sales leader. The first order of the day before he made his daily rounds was to make sure that he looked and felt good. Tailored suits, shiny shoes, well-combed hair and pleasing appearance were standards that must be followed starting with himself, day in day out.

This values served him well when he started McDonalds. His fastidious adherence to operating processes and procedures became standards in restaurant operations worldwide. He firmly believed that the quality of a leader is reflected in the standards he set for himself.

Motivator

What set Ray apart from his contemporaries was his ability to make people do willingly what he wanted them to do, although he is the type of a leader who would not ask anyone to do things that he himself is not willing or able to do. He's known to have mopped floors and clean toilets for franchisees during store openings in the early days of McDonalds.

Enthusiasm

A key to Ray's overall success is his infectious enthusiasm that attracted people to him. Whether they are potential franchisees, employees, suppliers or investors, he had a certain way of making people like him and to accept his ideas. Apparently, this ability helped him sell millions of paper cups to hard-nosed Italian and Polish restaurant owners in the streets of Chicago during his days as a salesman. He was considered a great storyteller, socializer, and had a way with words.

Mentor and Coach

Ray never finished high school but to me he is a great teacher. He liked and originated the idea of the "Hamburger University" that systematized the teaching of the ins and outs not only of preparing burgers and fries but running fast foods restaurants. Even before the concept of operations analysis became a buzzword in business circles and taught in the universities, it was already part of the curriculum in the training programs at McDonald's.

Optimist

Ray never wavered despite obstacles that come his way. For instance, when he was having a hard time perfecting the process of preparing potatoes - a big problem in the cold and damp weather of Des Plaines, Illinois but not in sunny San Bernardino,

California - instead of being discouraged, he embarked on a series of fact finding and research, until he found the solution.

This he did in many other situations he encountered in the early days of McDonalds. One of my favorites is the story of how he knew how many hamburgers his competitor across the street exactly sold each day. He "researched" by checking on the competitor's garbage cans in the dead of night, the night before!

Great Communicator

A salesman that he is, communication is one skill he does naturally and well. This is how he gets across his ideas, his vision and anything he wanted to tell people. And he does it with style, like having President Kennedy present in the inauguration of a store or by grabbing a microphone in the stadium when he wanted his San Diego Padres to play better!

The golden arches, which Ray adopted and became a de facto symbol of the American Dream, is one example of how he made use of communications as a powerful means of persuasion. He believed in it and made use of it to the fullest.

Then and now, when people see this symbol, an important entrepreneurial undertaking is taking place in any of the 18,710 restaurants anywhere in the world, 24 hours a day, seven days a week.

For the consumer, it says "hey drop by for some delicious and satisfying meals"! For the franchisee, more profits from the cash register.

MCDONALD'S PRODUCTS CONSISTENCY

The name McDonald itself brings water to the mouth because of their very tasty food menu and especially because of their hallmark burgers. Kids as well as adults from around the world love McDonalds and it is a breakfast as well as a fast food home to many. So what are the factors which make people love McDonalds so much?

1) The menu / Product Portfolio

McDonalds is the leading king in the burgers arena with the other king (burger king) not far behind. The reason for the success of McDonalds is that it is ready to diversify its products as per the country it enters. Thus, you will find the menu different in USA, UK as well as Asian countries. When you are ready to customize as per local taste, you will be hit locally. Thus, it is no doubt that McDonalds has 35000 outlets worldwide and a presence in 118 countries. So basically, if a single outlet sells 3 burgers a minute, Mcdonalds would probably sell 1 lakh burgers within a minute. So what else makes the McDonalds unbeatable?

2) Operations

Just think about the expansive operations which Mcdonalds needs to take to provide its burgers to so many people across the globe. Not only burgers, Mcdonalds has a tie up for many different food products. Many of these products are sourced from smaller companies who mass manufacture for the fast food giant. Similarly, beverages for instance are taken care of by Coca cola only and it is the sole supplier for all McDonald's outlets. Thus handling such large operations in itself is mind boggling and Mcdonalds does it perfectly.

3) Supply Chain

You will hardly ever hear a McDonalds say that they are out of stock and they cannot give you your favorite burger in time. This might happen over a very hectic weekend on peak of festivals. But other than that, McDonalds supply chain is flawless – from the procurement of raw material to the supply of the end product.

4) Franchise concept

Because McDonalds offers franchises, its growth has been very fast. The margins that McDonalds takes from franchises are high but at the same time, the brand as well as the product are always up to mark making the franchise concept a huge success for the brand. The layout of the store, the colors used and the overall ambiance is such that you feel home at a McDonalds across the world. Due to this concept, McDonalds finds a presence in 118 countries and it is growing stronger and faster than ever.

5) Consistency

McDonalds has always been a consistent brand, with strong focus on quality. This is one of the reasons that the brand has bounced back even after many controversies which point fingers at McDonalds. Bad experiences have happened with bad things being found in McDonald's food. However, this has not affected the brand globally and from a hiccup here or there, the company has always bounced back.

6) Brand elements

From colors of yellow and red, to advertising whenever a local outlet has opened, to the bright menu behind the Mcdonalds counter, to the chairs and tables which are polished and always in a specific layout, to the way people in a Mcdonalds always behave nicely, there are many brand elements which contribute towards making McDonalds an admired brand.

7) The happiest brand mascot ever

No one has as big a smile as Ronald McDonald. And why should the smile not be there? The company is growing successfully, children love the brand and so do adults. And we all love Ronald, don't we? Ronald is a friend to everyone at your local McDonalds outlet (He is often found sitting and smiling on a bench). At the same time, he is present across the globe and greets people on vacations and over the weekends.

HOW MCDONALD'S BUILD ITS SUSTAINABLE COMPETITIVE ADVANTAGE? -THE KEY SUCCESS FACTORS AND BUSINESS STRATEGY

The first step for any business is to ponder how to occupy space inside a consumer's mind, which is called 'Positioning'. It can also be termed as a consumer's perception of a brand with respect to competing brands. A customer would notice a brand only when there is a markable difference from other brands.

Michael Porter writes, "A company can outperform rivals only if it can establish a difference that it can preserve. It must offer greater value to customers or create comparable value at a lower cost, or do both"

What values did McDonald's offer in those initial years?

In the 1930s, the 'fast food' concept was spreading among the masses. A lot of drive-in restaurants sprouted in many places. The fast-food menu was revolving around Barbecue Beef, Pork and Chicken. Into this scenario, in the year 1937, two brothers Maurice and Richard McDonald started their own fast-food restaurant at San Bernardino. The business soon attracted a lot of teenagers and continued to grow rapidly.

The Hiccup -After world war II, the brothers felt that they were not making enough profits even though their parking lots were full all the time. They realized that one of the reasons was that they were selling too many items like every other competitor. Their resources were stretched to the limits, affecting the quality and the timely service.

The Reflection -McDonald brothers realized that their offerings were becoming like 'me-too' products. A product for everybody is like a product for nobody. Most 'me-too' products would fail to achieve reasonable sales after some time because their positioning is based on 'better than the competitor' rather than the 'Value to the customer'. McDonald brothers did not want to fall into the trap of becoming another 'me-too' product. They wanted to focus on providing something different, something valuable to the customer.

'Hamburger' was a common favorite food in America at that time. What value differentiation, McDonald brothers could provide?

VALUE PROPOSITIONS

Fast and Efficient -How about Quicker service to consumers? Quicker Service -Would it be possible to reduce the time taken to deliver? McDonald brothers realized that cutting down the number of items on the menu would free the resources to help in quicker delivery.

"It is better to do one product well than two products in a mediocre way," -Reed Hastings.

McDonald brothers decided to focus only on Hamburgers and its complimentary items. The menu became a shorter one.

Lean Process -To further reduce the time to deliver, the brothers copied lean-manufacturing process used in automobile companies and the war machines assembly units during the world war II.

Earlier, McDonald's used to prepare sandwiches in batches and keep them warm in ovens. This would reduce the serving time, but the wastage increased on the days when the demand was less. To deal with this, they then started to keep patties, salad and other ingredients ready, and combine them into finished sandwiches, only when an order is placed. The time taken during this process was only a few minutes, enabling a quick response to any change in demand. Inventory was also brought down. Thus the risk of wastage was eliminated.

They also began to develop assembly line machines to prepare hamburgers, French fries and beverages. The machines drastically reduced the time further. The tests showed that consumers were happy and pleasantly surprised when they received orders quickly.

Price -The assembly line machines brought down the labor cost too. As the machines delivered quickly, the volume of sales increased and further helped McDonald's to sell quality hamburger cheaper than other competitors.

Quality in Product -As the machines handled most of the tasks, McDonald brothers were free to work on the quality of the product at every step. That further enhanced the quality of Hamburgers, fries and beverages. They saw that competitors were mixing small quantities of other ingredients in the beef patties to save cost which was affecting the quality of their product. The brothers took responsibility to ensure that McDonald's would sell only one hundred per cent beef patties. No compromise on quality. Similarly, they took extra efforts to ensure that each patty would contain exactly nineteen percentage of fat content. Their French fries were better than any other competitor in the town.

Quality Experience -It is impossible to become a leading sustainable brand if the company's quality is associated with only the products. McDonald brothers not only focused on the quality of products, services and processes but also on the quality of infrastructure for enabling awesome experiences. They designed the store to enhance the quality of everything the customers see, touch, hear, smell and taste. The huge arches, the octagonal structure, glass partitions between kitchen & delivery areas and so on. They gave particular attention to 'Aroma' as it plays a vital role in the store experience. The premises were kept clean. The employees were trained to interact friendly with their customers. McDonald's was also about building experience environments.

Cleanliness -The chances of a customer turning loyal to a brand is high if he leaves the premises with a positive service experience about the brand. One of the factors that have the potential to hinder the positive service experience is Customer's hidden anxieties. It was important to address the elements and design every customer touch point in a way that would not trigger those anxieties in the customer.

McDonald brothers observed that one of the common worries of most of their customers was food hygiene and safety. They felt that it was important that none of the customer touch points should trigger this emotion -They took efforts to keep high standards of hygiene & cleanliness, in and around the restaurant. They made sure that employee's attire also would reflect hygiene and cleanliness. They motivated employees to adhere to the hygienic standards all the time. The customers were allowed to view the kitchen and the supporting areas where the food is prepared & processed.

So, McDonald's Value Propositions were Quicker Service, Lower Price, Quality Food, Quality Experience and Cleanliness. As per Porter's definition of Strategy, McDonald was offering both value and low price to customers.

SERVICE AS MANUFACTURING

When Ray Kroc took control of the McDonald's in the year 1955, he liked the McDonald's idea of comparing service and production to the concept of car assembly line and manufacturing process. He too began to view everything from the assembly line perspective. He felt that the process flow and the production assembly line could further be improved. Ray Kroc's past experiences(Worked in paper cup industry and also developed & sold multi-mixer machines) had also provided him with sufficient knowledge about process flow and equipment design.

Independent of Operators-To ensure repeat business, Ray Kroc believed that McDonald's has to provide a consistent experience across all outlets by standardizing the quality of food, speed of service, methods of preparation, environment and cleanliness. Like an assembly line in a product manufacturing company, Ray Kroc was trying to take the operator out of the equation and rely on the system's operations. Improving a service that depends on the performance of an operator would be inconsistent as people differ in attitudes, skills, interests, tastes, behaviors, experience and in environments where they grew up.

Operational Strategy -A business may have to perform hundreds of activities to create, produce, sell and deliver their products or services. Michael Porter says, "To establish a sustainable competitive advantage, a company has to perform some activities that are different from rivals and perform similar activities(Where it could not be avoided) in different ways.

Ray Kroc meticulously looked into each and every activity of McDonald's. He kept exploring the possibility of new ways of performing some of the activities and, better yet, pondered the possibility of actually changing the activity itself.

STANDARDISATION

As we have seen earlier, the way forward to provide consistent quality across all stores is not to depend on an operator's individual skills, ability and strengths. One of the solutions is to standardize the preparation of many ingredients as possible, particularly the core ingredients. Ray's team developed their own methods and equipment in preparing the ingredients without manual intervention. One of the examples is below

The raw hamburger patties are prepared and semi-cooked in a centralized place, without any manual intervention in determining the texture, thickness, density, consistency and color.

The patties are carefully prepacked and premeasured, which completely eliminates the possibility of any errors from a human operator. It was then delivered to the stores. This semi-processed food brought down the cooking time and enabled operators to deliver the end products in quick time.

The semi-cooked food dramatically lowered the wastage and helped to keep the store clean & hygienic with minimum effort. The cost of cooking the food and maintaining inventory also came down.

McDonald's designed and developed testing equipment to test and validate the quality of patties.

McDonald's have given this kind of attention to all major ingredients like French fries, buns etc..

Standardization of ingredients allowed to optimize storage, preparation space and related facilities for a predetermined mix of products, thereby saving time, minimizing wastage, and reducing the cost. It was difficult for an operator to introduce any new process or ingredient or product into this system. The operator was forced to sell whatever McDonald's corporation decides due to his facility limitations.

Standardization helped in high volume production and sales, and managers were able to forecast demand with high precision. It was easier to manage peak demands as the inventory management was made simple.

Standardization brought down the employees training cost. The repeatability of actions helped the employees to work faster on the production line without compromising the quality of the product.

LAYOUT

To deliver a good quality product in a quick time with a minimum price, Ray saw that layout design would play a major role. The key to good facility layout and design is the integration of customer's needs and employee's needs resulting in a smooth flow of materials, work and information. Ray's team worked on the layout to impart following benefits

It would be easy to interact with customers to take an order and deliver in quick time

The store employees would have everything in its reach to serve the customer quickly

Machines, product ingredients were arranged in such a way to create a single, well-functioning system

The layout was designed in such a way that it could be expanded by adding resources to meet the increased customer demands

As the customers could see inside the store, Ray wanted to use it a promotional value for McDonald's. The store facility layout with machines, storage boxes had to be laid out in an attractive way that would further increase the value of the brand.

To optimize the space and provide more ventilation.

To control the climatic conditions inside the store during summer and winter.

The Equipments were placed in such a way that the number of steps involved in performing the task would be reduced.

EQUIPMENT

Ray Kroc and his team were constantly looking for ways to reduce the number of steps involved in performing the task, skill level needed and the time consumed. Having worked in a multi-mixer industry, he felt that machines would solve those major problems and also bring down the product's cost thereby establishing a massive competitive advantage. At the same time, he firmly believed that equipment had to be energy efficient, easy to clean, easy to use, and importantly, provide consistent taste. Food made with the help of machine was also considered more hygienic at that time.

Jim Schindler, one of Ray Kroc's associates, was called a steel magician. He had spent years in designing and developing food processing machines. In the earlier years of McDonald, Jim had worked overtime to ensure that the right equipment was made and also, the machines were easy to use.

Earlier McDonald's was making milkshakes with a hand dipping ice-cream method, which was a time-consuming process and the quality was operator-dependent. Jim Schindler modified it using a pre-measured ice-cream drawn from the overhead tank, improving the productivity and consistency.

Ray's team also developed high-efficiency fryers which would drastically reduce the time to fry the chips. The fryer machine also simplified filtering and cleaning, thereby improving the taste and also provided enhanced environmental benefits. The machine consumed 40% less oil than the normal manual process. McDonald's implemented a conveyor system, a radical step in a fast food industry at that time.

Jim's team kept working on a lot of other machines to improve productivity, quality, thereby enhancing the service experience and earning more revenue. Ray Kroc invested in machines well ahead of his competitors.

BUNS

Buns are such an important part of McDonald's business that prompted Ray's team to devote special attention. They not only worked on the texture, form, size of the bun but also looked at them from the assembly line perspective. Initially, the buns were delivered to stores in clusters of four to six with partially being sliced. One of Ray's team associate Fred Turner saw that it would be easier and faster for a griddle man if McDonald's received individual buns rather than clusters. The buns supplier was asked to slice the buns all the way through to the bottom. This drastically reduced the preparation time and speeded up the service. The preparation area was also left a lot less messy.

INGREDIENTS PACKAGING

Ray's associate Fred Turner kept working on the packaging of semi-processed foods and other ingredients, as they had to be transported from the assembly location to individual stores. Earlier, the buns being made as a cluster had been using a lot of papers and the kitchen ended up messier with papers thrown around. A lot of time was also lost in opening up packages. Fred designed a sturdy, reusable cardboard box for holding individual buns. It was easy to handle, transport and reduced shipping costs. Fred kept refining the cardboard box. He modified the box by extending the top lid all the way to the bottom so that it can hold moisture for a long time. Through experiments, he figured out that an extra heavy coating of wax inside the box would increase the number of reuses from the box.

Fred also worked on the packaging of patties, an essential component of McDonald's business. He did a lot of experiments before arriving at the right kind of paper for packaging, with the right kind of wax which would enable the patty to pop out without sticking when the griddle man slaps it into the griddle. He optimized the size of the box based on the science of stacking patties without messing up the bottom-most patty.

Fred looked at every activity that would help griddle man's job easier and worked on it. He extended the principle to every other ingredient and designed a suitable packaging.

McDonald continues to monitor various other activities with an emphasis on reducing its cost and time without compromising the quality.

BRANDING -TAKEAWAY PACKAGING

Ray Kroc gave particular importance to customer's takeaway packaging as it was visible to both customers & non-customers and also had the potential to represent quality, integrity and safety of the brand. He chose good quality paper material for takeaways. In 1961, he modified the graphics in the packaging and for the first time, he gave prominence to McDonald's famous arches(The customers were already familiar with arches and Ray Kroc thought that it would be better to exploit this familiarity) to aid in brand recognition & recall.

Rather than the words, symbols would communicate effectively at a glance, even from a far away distance. Nowadays, we could see the arches that are positioned to be clearly visible to passing motorists in the highways. It's a sign that signifies an assured, known quality food. The symbol quickly conveys a story. They do not need words or a tagline.

The foremost task in promoting a brand is to make it clear where it would be available. McDonalds' arch is so effective in this case.

FRENCH-FRYING OPERATION

One of the key elements in McDonald's success was 'french-fry operation'. Many of the Kroc's close suppliers had commented to him that McDonald's was not in hamburger business at all but in the french-fry business.

Marketing Tool -McDonald brothers realized in their earlier days that they had the best of french-fries in the town and it brought customers back to the store. They began to give special attention to the french-fries when every other competitor thought that french-fried potato is a necessary evil and an uninspiring one whose function was just to kill the time. But for McDonald brothers, it was the main marketing tool -they gave special attention to it. The preparation process was a ritual for them.

Immerse Yourself -Ray Kroc, when he took over the McDonald's, loved the french-frying ritual. He himself took part in peeling, washing, blanching and cooking of french-fries. He purchased good quality fresh potatoes directly from the farmers -He carefully stored them in double layered mesh bins in order to let the fresh air in but keep the rats & critters away.

Obtaining Consistent Quality -In the late 1950s, Ray Kroc observed that potato peelings were giving plenty of problems in some of the stores. Peeling and blanching was a time-consuming process and also made the place messier. Some of the operators were finding it difficult to replicate the blanching process. Disposal of wastewater from the process posed another challenge in some places as the soil conditions were not conducive enough to absorb the water. There was a terrible stinking smell emanating from the wastewater accumulation.

To standardize the taste and quality of french-fries in all the stores, Ray Kroc began to standardize and automate many of the processes. He devised machines to peel the potato, carefully leaving a tiny portion of thin skin on, before cutting them into long pieces, while taking the operator's skills out of the system. McDonald brothers used a natural curing process in their open bins as they were staying in a desert area and got a good breeze. Ray realized that relying on natural environment would be a disaster for the brand at some places. His team then devised an artificial curing system in the 1950s, using a big electric fan. They automated the time to allow for sugars change to starch.

In the year 1962, two of Ray Kroc's associates developed an idea of using frozen potatoes that drastically changed McDonald's business. Now the corporation could supply its outlets with precut, semi-cooked frozen potatoes that could be quickly cooked in a store using a deep-dry facility.

No more stinking smells, no more wastewater disposal problems, no more messy stores.

Fryer Equipment -Theodore Levit, in his HBR article, writes that the McDonald's fryer at the store is neither so large that it produces too many French fries at one time (thus allowing them to become soggy) nor so small that it requires frequent and costly frying. The fryer was designed to consume 40% less oil.

Tray and The Scoop Handle - The fryer is emptied onto a wide, flat tray adjacent to the service counter. This tray is designed and located in such a way to avoid spillage while filling the french-fries to the brim of the bag in order to give an impression of abundance and generosity. Ray Kroc's team designed the scoop handle that would fill french-fries in exact portions in the delivery bag without soiling the employee's hands or dress or the environment.

Ray's team optimized each and every activity of french-frying process when the competitors were not giving enough attention to the product itself.

TRADEOFFS

McDonald's owes their initial success to a unique strategic position involving clear trade-offs. Choosing a unique activity or a differentiation is not enough to guarantee a sustainable competitive advantage as competing brands could easily copy or imitate those value propositions and unique activities. But they would find it difficult to copy one thing—The Trade-offs.

Trade-offs are the activities a brand chooses not to do, the activities that would be incompatible with the brand's vision and core values.

Without trade-offs, there would be no choice and thus no need for strategy—Michael Porter.

The desire to grow puts enormous pressure on the business owners and they make some compromises. They add a series of incremental changes which lead them to lose their way.

-In the year 1948, McDonald brothers began to focus only on Hamburgers, French fries and the related items. They decided to focus and expand their energy only on their core strengths.

-Everywhere Hamburger patty is a piece of meat but in McDonald's, it was a piece of meat with a soul. From the beginning, they were hell-bent on maintaining one hundred percentage beef in the patties. They never allowed mixing anything in the grounded beef mixture while the competitors were mixing things in beef patties to save cost. The competitors had also put holes in the patties like a doughnut and plugged the hole with pickles or other ingredients. But McDonald's never compromised on their quality. They developed tests to strictly maintain the prescribed nineteen percentage fat content.

-McDonald's refrained from selling Pizzas as they thought that it would affect their core strengths and core values.

-In the year 1960s and 1970s, many of the stores were earning an extra income through pay telephones, jukeboxes and other types of vending machines. Being tempted by those extra profits, many operators approached Ray Kroc to allow those machines. But Ray Kroc stayed firm and never allowed. He felt that it would create unproductive traffic in the store and create inconvenience to core-customers, affecting the brand's core values. It would downgrade the family image, which McDonald's was trying to portray.

The Benefits-By delivering one kind of value, McDonald's projected an image of consistency whereas his competitors were confusing their customers. McDonald's reputation grew. This trade-off showed its employees how the McDonald's management is seriously committed to the brand's core values. It made the organizational priorities clear to all its employees. It helped the brand to build a strong internal brand culture.

McDonald's, by choosing not to do some of the activities, projected a consistent image of credibility and built a sustainable competitive advantage.

HIRE RIGHT PEOPLE

A founder alone cannot build a sustainable brand. He or she would build a great company if he or she could find a colleague who had 'shared common interests' and who could bring different strengths to the company.

"If you have the right people, then the problem of how to motivate and how to manage people properly goes away"-Jim Collins

Ray Kroc, while recruiting employees, made sure that he chose people who shared his passion, commitment and goals. He believed that like-minded souls would create a far greater impact.

One of Ray Kroc's earliest hires, Mrs. June Martino was from a poor family and was struggling to meet ends, before she joined McDonald's. Ray saw that she exhibited a compassionate personality and had a natural persistence to deal with the problems. Ray hired her despite she having no book-keeping experience. In the next twenty years, she grew to the position of secretary and treasurer of McDonald's corporation. She was voted as one of the top women executives in America.

Ray's one of the successful hires, Ed McLuckie was a friend's son-in-law. But he hired him because he was passionate about the food service business. He became one of his successful store operators.

Art Bender was McDonald brother's successful hires. Art Bender was a musician and was also doing part-time work in making sodas, ice-creams and milk-shakes. He loved both the professions. After some time, he started the fast food business but lost everything and become broke. He then joined a restaurant as an employee and worked day & night in supplying sandwiches and ice-cream. Mac McDonald, who visited the restaurant often, liked Art Bender's work ethics, cleanliness and the way he performed the tasks sincerely. After he heard that Art Blender had already gone broke, he immediately hired him for McDonald's. Art Blender served the first hamburger of McDonald's in 1948. Art Blender helped Ray to open more stores, train employees and help the operators in sourcing materials etc...

Another of Ray's earlier hires, Fred Turner was from a wealthy family. He approached Ray to buy a franchise. Ray liked Fred's problem-solving ability, attention to details and his passion for the work. Fred began his McDonald's career by working as an employee in one of the stores, cooking, cleaning and serving the customers. Fred solved a lot of operational problems in McDonald's franchises. He became the operations-in-charge and later he became CEO.

Harry Sonneborn, another Ray's earlier played a major role in McDonald's expansion. Before joining McDonald's, he was working as V.P of Tastee-Freeze, an ice-cream chain. Harry was inspired by Ray's vision, his hands-on working and wanted to join McDonald's to take part in its growth. When Ray met Harry, he felt that both of them spoke the same language of business and passion. Though Ray made it clear that he had no money to pay him, Harry was resolute and persistent, the qualities which Kroc liked very much. It was not the money which motivated people to join McDonald's.

FRANCHISING

The desire for growth forced every other competitor of McDonald's to expand quickly through the franchising route as it was the logical, quick and easy way to raise capital. The problem was that most of them could not control the quality at any of their franchises and eventually ran themselves out of the business. Even McDonald brothers were happy to sell franchise license but not interested in following up through and maintaining checks. But Ray Kroc was not interested in compromising the quality of their franchises. Superior techniques, standardization, employee & operator training programmes and frequent monitoring helped franchises to deliver uniform quality.

Harry Sonneborn was in-charge of developing franchises who himself had learnt the pitfalls of franchising from his earlier job at Tastee-Freeze ice-cream chain. Those lessons helped McDonald's to maintain high standards in every franchise.

A franchise is not your customer -Every other competitor saw their franchises as a money-making machine. They sold machines, ingredients to their franchises and also took a share in their revenues along with a license fee. From the beginning, Ray was clear that the corporation was not going to be a supplier for its operators. He felt that there was a basic conflict in seeing a franchise as part of the organization and at the same time, seeing them as a customer, trying to sell something and make a profit out of them. He was very clear that the corporation should try its best to help an operator to succeed in his business and should not be concerned about how much the company would be going to sell to him or her.

The company encourages every store operator to find their own supply sources within that area and also would help the potential vendors to build automated systems to produce and supply the ingredients at a low cost. The experience of McDonald's executives simplifies a lot of work for an operator. The McDonald's executives would work with the vendors to get the required quality, texture and consistency of buns, meat and other condiments. They also train the vendors and impart them the ways each ingredient need to be packed and supplied to individual stores.

Selection of an Operator -Whenever somebody approached Ray Kroc to buy a franchise, he would check whether he or she would be totally committed to run the franchise and whether he or she would be willing to work hard and concentrate exclusively on the challenges of operating the store. He had asked every potential candidate to work for hundreds of hours in one of the McDonald's stores without conflicting their personal work at that stage. Once the candidate gained sufficient knowledge and skills, he would be given proper orientation training -he would be taught about the operations, the art of influencing people, management and leadership skills.

Locations -Ray and Harry would hunt the store locations on their own, lease them and rent it to franchises for a period of twenty years. Franchise owner rarely had an opportunity to choose their own location. This way, McDonald's controlled everything as the place was owned by them and not by the operator.

The McDonald's model was the first successful one in developing large-scale franchise network with consistent experiences across all locations.

REAL ESTATE STRATEGY

Harry Sonneborn, Former McDonald's CFO said, " "We are not technically in the food business. We are in the real estate business. The only reason we sell fifteen-cent hamburgers is that they are the greatest producer of revenue, from which our tenants can pay us our rent."

Observational Research -As Ray's team had the knowledge and experience in running McDonald's stores, they chose the franchise locations. They spotted good locations by flying over the community and looked for schools and church steeples from above. Once they zoned in on a promising location, Ray and Harry would move around the location by walk and by car. They would visit nearby shops, supermarket stores, salons, spend time there and observe the movement of people and their behaviors. Both of them would check out traffic flows, which way cities and towns would be growing, would evaluate the best ways to transport goods to & from the store, and assess the location of possible competition. They did thorough research before finalizing the location.

Right Time with Right Skill -Initially, Ray & Harry built franchises mainly in suburbs. Most of the earlier locations were nothing but a bare ground, where the owner would be happy to rent it out. Both Harry and Ray were being a good salesman, it was easy for them to convince property owners to lend out space. In the late 1950s and the early

1960s, a lot of vacant lands were available as the franchise business was yet to proliferate on a large scale. Ray Kroc was lucky to be expanding the business in a period of less fierce competition.

Being In Control Of Business -It was Sonneborn's idea to have the McDonald's company lease a plot of land and the building for each restaurant. The company would then sublease to the franchisee that would run the restaurant. Harry took classes on the fundamentals of leasing and also hired a professional attorney to help him in the lease agreements.

Investments -For the proposed idea to work, Sonneborn needed a large amount of money. He had good contacts with many of the insurance companies and roped in some of them to pay for the mortgages of those plots and the building. Without those investments, McDonald's would not have grown faster.

The other competitors never owned the land and whatever the investments they acquired were only through the franchise fee which was not sufficient enough to let them invest in a large-scale assembly line production plant and new technologies.

HAMBURGER UNIVERSITY

Another major reason why McDonald's could provide consistent quality food, maintain a clean environment and make customers leave with a smile was their employees. Employees are responsible for the wonderful customer experiences and McDonald's training programmes under Hamburger University played a major role.

Ray Kroc, started Hamburger University in the year 1961 -the world's first restaurant company to open a 'Global Training Center'. It was surprising to know that Ray and his executive team thought well ahead in those times and implemented the 'University' idea. The concept of 'Corporate Universities' sprouted mostly in the last thirty years. Ray Kroc got a massive head-start.

The university was started with the sole aim to provide a decent future for McDonald's employees. The employees were not only trained extensively in the McDonald's operations but also in social skills, restaurant leadership and business leadership. The university also taught them ethics, accountability and responsibility. It was a platform to help employees to climb the career ladder inside the McDonald's. It helped the franchise owners and managers dramatically in successfully running the franchise business.

RESEARCH AND DEVELOPMENT LABORATORY

In the year 1961, Ray Kroc established McDonald's Research and Development laboratory with the help of Louis Martino. Louis, an engineer had worked as an operator and felt that the McDonald's operations needed more sophisticated automated equipment to standardize the products and speed up the whole process. This lab kept working on new innovations, new types of equipment and new technology.

-While making french-fries, potatoes had to be pulled out of oil when they got a certain color uniformly. But it was a subjective one as each person would have his own interpretation and this affected the quality of french-fries. Louis's team developed a computer program to pull out potatoes automatically when it got the color. They also automated the timing of the blanching process. They automated many processes through computer programming. They automated the frying time to suit the balance of water to solids in a given batch of potatoes. They devised automated dispenser systems to dole out the right amount of Catsup and Mustard into hamburger patties. They designed testing equipment like Fatiliyzer to validate the nineteen percentage fat content in the hamburger.

McDonald's was investing in computers, technology and research while the competitors were unwilling to bet on them.

New Product Development -McDonald's R&D also observe the behavioral change in the customers, the signs of fatigue in the taste monotony, and the changing food trends. They conduct ethnographic research, including shadowing customers and gather insights into how McDonald's could help consumers in their everyday lives. Based on the research data, they continue to innovate new products, test them and launch it in the market. McMuffin, Big Mac, Breakfast Sandwiches, Apple Pie were all the results of McDonald's R&D lab's efforts. The lab also understands the nation-specific customer behavior, cultural requirements, taste preferences and help McDonald's to customize their product offerings. In India, they have McAloo Tikki Burger, Spicy Paneer Wrap and so on. -Customized food, catering to the needs of Indian taste buds.

Investing in R&D right from the beginning became a vital factor for McDonald's sustained leadership in the market.

OPERATORS NATIONAL ADVERTISING FUND(OPNAD)

Until the early 1970s, McDonald's was expanding exclusively in the suburbs. A few of the stores were struggling to attract customers. When Ray gave advertisements in the national media, he saw that those stores began to increase customer foot-print rapidly.

In the late 1950s and early 1960s, many fast food stores saw the money paid for advertisement programs or publicity campaigns were expenditures. But Ray Kroc saw it as an investment and he believed that the benefits came in many forms like building brand recognition, brand recall etc... In 1957, he hired an expensive public relations firm for $500 a month while he was struggling to pay salaries for himself and his employees. His investments in advertisements from the beginning helped McDonald's rapid expansion in the minds of customers.

Ray Kroc set up a fund called Operators National Advertising Fund, where every store would contribute a small Percentage of gross to advertising campaigns. This led to volume purchasing of advertisement slots. Centralized advertising programmes further led to cost savings per consumer gained. It was a wonderful bargain for individual stores. It would be expensive for a store to hire external agencies to make those quality advertisements on their own.

Ray Kroc also helped operators to form a local association within their state and contribute One Percent to advertise in their local market. He encouraged them to hire their own local agencies, run their own campaigns in those markets by following guidelines established by the McDonald's corporation.

The advertisements benefitted every store and helped the brand to grow quicker than other competitors.

EMBRACE AND DRIVE CHANGE

It is a well-known fact that every business must learn to adapt to their changing environment to remain successful. As long as the company remains close to their customers, they would find solutions to the questions 'What to be changed? and 'When to change?'.

The way to adapt to a changing environment is to anticipate and act in advance than reacting to the change. One of the solutions is to Innovate. Innovation is possible through an integrated process of experimentation. Through literally thousands of small experiments, McDonald's refined it's new products, then tested them, made sure that it meets the quality standards and then, they had launched it.

"The most important and visible outcropping of the action bias in the excellent companies is their willingness to try things out, to experiment."—From the book 'In Search Of Excellence'.

Fillet-O-Fish Sandwich -Once, operator of one of the store franchises, Lou observed that people in his area had developed a taste preference for fish based products and some of the local sellers had begun to sell products to meet those demands. Backed by research data, Lou's team convinced Ray Kroc to try a fish sandwich. They experimented every detail -Type of fish, type of breeding, how long to cook, how thick it should be, how soft it has to be, kind of sauce that would be best for the product, and they continued experimenting with many other ingredients. While experimenting, they discovered that by adding cheese, the fish sandwich became delicious. Finally, Fillet-O-Fish was born. McDonald's launched it and saw that sales rocketed through the roof.

Hot Apple Pie -After observing customers for some time, McDonald's research team found that many customers were desperately looking for a dessert item after the meals. They experimented with the type of dessert that would fit readily into the existing assembly line system and also gain wide acceptance among the common customers. They experimented with Strawberry shake, Pound cake, Kolackies, brownies but nothing caught up with the consumers. Then, one fine day, McDonald's experimented with an Apple Pie recipe received from one of the operator's mother. The team changed the frying methods, ingredients, type of apples used, the hardness of the external crust, the viscosity of the hot sweet fillings inside, sugar levels and so on. They market-tested the product and later, they launched it. It was a resounding success and going strong even after fifty years.

Egg McMuffin -In the late 1960s, some of the operators were looking for ways to bring more business during the morning hours. The McDonald's team experimented with simple breakfast items. One of the operators, Herb Peterson took a commonly available Eggs Benedict Sandwich and began experimenting. He changed various ingredients, added cheese, tried other combinations and tested various consistencies. While experimenting, he complimented the egg and muffin with grilled bacon and that transformed customer's experience. McDonald's breakfast business took off and soon was growing in double digits.

The company continued to invent & introduce more breakfast items in the early 1970s while the brand's competitors began to introduce commercial breakfast items only in the mid-1980s. McDonald's got a massive head-start.

McDonald's continued to experiment and innovate and launched many products like Big Mac, Shamrock Shake, larger size fries, Happy Meals for kids, Cherry Pie and so on which went on to help McDonald's build strong brand loyalty.

SUPPLY CHAIN MANAGEMENT

McDonald's supply chain owes its success to Ray Kroc's long-term vision. A vision that would profit everyone in the supply chain-Customers, Operators, Employees, Vendors and the Corporation.

Vendors as Partners -Ray saw vendors as business partners. He preferred to build a long-term relationship with every vendor and he chose vendors who were passionate and shared his vision. Many of McDonald's supply chain vendors have been around from the beginning.

McDonald's executives spend time with their vendors to find better, faster and cheaper ways to deliver McDonald's core values.

They also help vendors with solutions if they encounter any production-related problems.

McDonald's plans the supply chain strategy along with their vendors.

The suppliers are encouraged to innovate and would be aptly rewarded.

One of the vendors, Martin-Brower Company LLC began supplying paper napkins in the year 1956 and it is now a multi-billion dollar company delivering products to more than McDonald's 15,000 locations in North America. The company kept innovating and added value to McDonald's customers. It has exclusive distribution centers, warehouses, logistics network for McDonald's.

Communication -One of the strong points of McDonald's Vendor relationship programme is the transparent and real-time communication of data. Communication is the key to collaboration. The company constantly tracked every sale, inventory, future customer demands and shared all data with partners, franchise owners. It also invested in systems to track the movement of ingredients in the logistics network.

Sourcing -McDonald's is the largest purchaser of beef globally and they directly buy from farmers ensuring the quality of meat. They also buy potatoes directly from the farmers. They never outsourced procurement process. They train in-house people to handle it. McDonald's contribute a lot to the welfare of farmers through education, technical knowledge and financial support. This helped them to build trust and forge a long-term relationship with farmers. McDonald 's made long-term contracts at fixed prices which helped them to gain protection against unknown events and price fluctuations. This was mutually beneficial.

Economics of Scale -As McDonald's restaurant buy more buns, more mustard, more catsup, the vendor who gets an opportunity to supply them consider it as a break of a lifetime. Moreover, the McDonald's executives would spend the time to help the vendor to lower the costs in every step. In the year 1955, Ray Kroc, for his first McDonald's store, chose Louis Kuchuris' Mary Ann Bakery as the supplier of buns. In the next fifteen years, Kuchuris built an automatic bun bakery, exclusively for McDonald's and served more than 40 stores in an area. They had a quarter mile long belt conveyor for cooling buns. The firm used one million pounds of flour per month. They also had an exclusive trucking company that serviced McDonald's stores. Due to the volume of sales, the vendors are ready to experiment McDonald's new requirements. When Fred Turner approached the supplier to change the supply of cluster of buns to individual ones, the vendors could afford to do that. Similarly, with the box packaging suppliers, the volume allowed McDonald's executives to experiment the packaging design and the vendors could implement those changes. The company is always engaged in an extensive utilization of economies of scale to achieve the cost advantage and better quality.

Cold Chain System -The perishable nature of products has forced McDonald's to adopt cold chain processing, storage and distribution across all levels of the supply chain system. The first fast-food chain to implement such a system. The cold chain maintained shelf-life, freshness and nutritional value of the product. It also brought down the cost considerably as the company could buy raw materials in bulk and process them in volumes. The distribution centers are equipped to handle multiple temperature requirements of different items.

Technology -McDonald's kept investing in computers and software. It's integrated IT system helps stores in real-time monitoring, ordering, procurement and tracking of deliveries. It also helps in seamless communication within the supply chain system between warehouses or distribution centers or trucks and store managers. The constant communication also helps to manage the inventory more accurately.

Inventory -As the value of materials declines rapidly, inventory was the worst thing to own in business. McDonald's runs a lean-process based assembly line to deliver products to the customer. The company designed the assembly process to meet instant demand, thereby reducing storage costs while minimizing wastage. Good vendor relationships also helped McDonald's to maintain lower inventory levels.

McDonald's restaurants have developed a reasonably accurate program for forecasting demand which further helps in inventory control. So, the McDonald's system has evolved over a period of time to keep less inventory all the time.

THE FUTURE OF MCDONALD'S

McDonald's outlined a long-term growth plan that will focus on convenience and technology in an attempt to win customers from competing quick-service restaurants.

Following the company's investor day on March 1, McDonald's announced it will launch mobile order and pay in 20,000 restaurants by the end of 2017, and that it will continue to accelerate its growth in delivery.

"As customers' expectations increased, McDonald's simply didn't keep pace with them," the company says in a statement. "Making meaningful improvements in quality, convenience, and value will win back some of McDonald's best customers."

The brand will also accelerate deployment of its "Experience of the Future" restaurant design in the U.S., which contains kiosk ordering and table service, increasing functionality with the mobile app, and a "more modern, more exciting restaurant environment." Through the mobile order and pay feature, McDonald's says its customers will also be able to skip the drive thru and choose curbside delivery. If customers choose the drive thru, they will read the already placed order code from the app and the order will be ready for pickup at the window.

McDonald's plans to reimage around 650 restaurants in 2017 to the Experience of the Future model, and when combined with previously modernized restaurants, the U.S. will have around 2,500 locations. By the end of 2020, the company intends to have most of its U.S. free-standing restaurants updated to this design.

"To deliver sustained growth, we have to attract more customers, more often," president and CEO Steve Easterbrook says in a statement. "Our greatest opportunities reside at the very heart of our brand—our food, value, and the customer experience."

McDonald's says it is "uniquely positioned to become the global leader in delivery." In its top five markets, nearly 75 percent of the population lives within 3 miles of a location.

"Going digital is McDonald's' most recent push to lure customers back to its stores. Digital engagement is an increasingly important aspect of the modern foodservice experience and it enhances the level of convenience that consumers want and expect from a quick-service chain. Digital channels, whether through self-service kiosks, mobile ordering, or even delivery, help make the chain more accessible, and should be a positive driver of traffic."

"Through enhanced technology to elevate and modernize the customer experience, a focus on the quality and value of our food and redefined convenience through delivery, we have a bold vision for the future and the urgency to act on it," Easterbrook says. "We are moving with velocity to drive profitable growth and becoming an even better McDonald's serving more customers delicious food each day around the world."

CONCLUSION

No matter where you are in the world, you can be certain that when you walk into a McDonald's you're going to have a familiar experience in terms of the menu, food wrapping and design of the building. In 1961 Ray Kroc launched the Hamburger University as a training school that emphasizes "consistent restaurant operations procedures, service, quality and cleanliness." Today, franchisees attend the program to learn and implement Ray Kroc's vision.

Research has proven that these types of programs not only enforce consistency, but can also increase productivity.

McDonald's has done an excellent job at establishing a brand presence. But beyond the "Golden Arches" and "I'm Lovin' It" slogan, McDonald's has created an emotional experience that takes us back to our childhood. Even though we realize that there are better products out there, most of us have a bond with McDonald's that is almost unbreakable -- which is why you hear so many people proclaim their love for McDonald's fries. The fries have a look and taste that you will find exactly the same no matter where you are in the world. You can count on it.

A strong brand presence helps your business build credibility and memories with your customers that will convert them into lifelong advocates. If you're struggling with your brand, here are a few tips to brand your company better.

Even though McDonald's practices consistency, the company isn't afraid to take risks and tinker with their menu. The original menu only included a hamburger, cheeseburger, fries, shake and beverages. Over the years, the chain has added breakfast items, the Happy Meal, McNuggets, (and 'Mc' everything else. Does this remind you of the 'I' we see everywhere on multiple iTems?) Filet-O-Fish, salads and the McRibs.

While there have been failures like the McLobster and McPizza, without taking those risks, McDonald's probably would not have grown into the global juggernaut that we know of today.

The reason that McDonald's is willingly to take risks is that the company realizes that it's vital to adapt to the needs and wants of customers. For example, the company scrapped the Super Size option and began offering healthier options as more people have become more health conscience. Additionally, the company also offers regional items based on local favorites.

However, the greatest adaptation was back in 1975. A McDonald's located near a military base in Arizona offered the first drive-thru to serve soldiers who were not allowed to leave their vehicles while wearing fatigues.

Cross-selling is when you take the product you're going to buy and co-promote other products with it. Sound familiar? It should. McDonald's has arguably the most famous cross-sell of all-time, "Would you like fries with that?"

This is great way to increase sales, but make sure that you don't overwhelm the customer. Wait for them to order first, gain more information about the sale and realize why it adds value to the final purchase. Another effective example of this is Amazon's "Frequently Bought Together" feature. And how about the effective cross-sell off, "Those who searched for this, (item, book, shirt, shoe, baby item), also searched for these six other items."

Employee's at McDonald's have to not only work with the public but also know how to work with colleagues. While congenial working and speaking with one another situations are valuable for essentially every business out there, many former McDonald's employees will inform you that this careful treatment of each other attributed to their success.

Ohio Congresswoman Marcia Fudge discovered that her time at McDonald's gave her the ability to "size up people's concerns, guide them through the process, apologize if something went wrong -- and hold your ground if someone's stopped being reasonable."

McDonald's also gives leaders the opportunity to help their team member succeed. While as a McDonald's manager Andrew Card, chief of staff for President George W. Bush, stated that "My job was determining how I could help each kid succeed." If an employee wasn't happy or skilled on the grill, the manager could move to cash register in order to tap into their strengths and preferences.

Did you know that 40 percent of McDonald's executives actually began as hourly employees? That's because the company knows how to spot talent and tap into the "hidden talents" of employees. McDonald's then rewards these employees by allowing them to work their way-up. It not only reduces turnover, but also builds a company that is full of employees who know the business inside and out and are extremely loyal. More importantly, however, this creates a company that is committed to one shared vision.

McDonald's is also known for giving back to the community through the Ronald McDonald House Charities, college scholarships, fundraisers and mentorship programs. McDonald's, like so many other philanthropic businesses, have realized that giving back is just good for business. By sharing the same values with customers, businesses can create loyal advocates and increase their revenue.

www.ingramcontent.com/pod-product-compliance
Lightning Source LLC
Chambersburg PA
CBHW081014170526
45158CB00010B/3033